K-15/M System

SOVIET SUPERSONIC ALL-WEATHER INTERCEPTOR COMPLEX

HUGH HARKINS

Copyright © 2019 Hugh Harkins

All rights reserved.

ISBN: 1-903630-84-3
ISBN-13: 978-1-903630-84-6

K-15/M System

Soviet Supersonic All-Weather Interceptor Complex

© Hugh Harkins 2019

Published by Centurion Publishing
United Kingdom

ISBN 10: 1-903630-84-3
ISBN 13: 978-1-903630-84-6

This volume first published in 2019

The Author is identified as the copyright holder of this work under sections 77 and 78 of the Copyright Designs and Patents Act 1988

Cover design © Centurion Publishing & KDP
Page layout, concept and design © Centurion Publishing

All rights reserved. No part of this publication may be reproduced, stored in a retrieval system, transmitted in any form, or by any means, electronic, mechanical or photocopied, recorded or otherwise, without the written permission of the publisher

The publisher and author would like to thank all organisations and services for their assistance and contributions in the preparation of this volume: A.C. Yakovlev OKB; Central Museum of the Aerospace Forces – Russian Federation Air Force Museum, Monino; Characteristic Summary (1954) 'Guided Aircraft Rocket GAR-1', Authority of Secretary of the Air Force; Characteristic Summary (1972), 'AGM-28A, US DoD; JSC Fazotron-NIIR; JSC Klimov; JSC NIIP V. Tikhomirov (JSC 'Research Institute for Instrument Engineering, V.V. Tikhomirov); JSC Sukhoi; JSC Tupolev; Ministry of Defence of the Russian Federation; National Museum of the United States Air Force; NPO Saturn; Russian Aircraft Corporation; Scientific and Production Association, S.A. Lavochkin; Standard Aircraft Characteristic (1959), 'B/RB-58A', Secretary of the Air Force

Citation guide: A.C. Yakovlev OKB (Yakovlev); Central Museum of the Aerospace Forces – Russian Federation Air Force Museum, Monino (Monino); Characteristic Summary (1954) 'Guided Aircraft Rocket GAR-1', Authority of Secretary of the Air Force (CS GAR-1, 1954); Characteristic Summary (1972), 'AGM-28A, US DoD (AGM-28A CS, 1972); JSC Fazotron-NIIR (Fazotron-NIIR); JSC NIIP V. Tikhomirov (JSC 'Research Institute for Instrument Engineering, V.V. Tikhomirov) (NIIP V. Tikhomirov); JSC Sukhoi (Sukhoi); JSC Tupolev (Tupolev); Ministry of Defence of the Russian Federation (MODRF); National Museum of the United States Air Force (NMUSAF); Russian Aircraft Corporation (RAC); Scientific and Production Association, S.A. Lavochkin (Laspace); Standard Aircraft Characteristic (1959), 'B/RB-58A', Secretary of the Air Force (SAC B/RB-58A, 1959); Harkins, H. (2013) *F-84 Thunderjet: Republic Thunder*, Centurion Publishing, United Kingdom; Harkins, H. (2018) Cold War Air Combats, USAF F-84E and Czechoslovak Air Force MiG-15 – West German Czechoslovak Border Region, 10 March 1952, Centurion Publishing, United Kingdom (Harkins, 2018) & Harkins, H. (2019) *XF-103: Mach 3 Mesospheric Interceptor Concept*, Centurion Publishing, United Kingdom (Harkins, 2018)

CONTENTS

	INTRODUCTION	vii
1	K-15/M SYSTEM – SOVIET EMBRYONIC ALL-WEATHER INTERCEPTION SYSTEM	1
2	GLOSSARY	26

INTRODUCTION

This research paper is intended to provide an overview of the early Soviet efforts to field an all-weather interceptor capability, leading to the OKB-301 K-15/M System. This emerged as the first Soviet airborne interception complex to be developed as an integrated weapon system, capable of conducting fully-automated interceptions against an aggressor nations strategic bomber fleets operating against the Soviet Union's northern and eastern boundaries. To facilitate destruction of the target the K-15M System was to employ air launched guided missiles armed with conventional and nuclear warheads.

All textual technical-historical data and graphic material has been furnished by various design and manufacturing bureau and the Ministry of Defense of the Russian Federation, with additional input form agencies and industries outside the Russian Federation.

1

K-15 SYSTEM – SOVIET EMBRYONIC SUPERSONIC ALL-WEATHER INTERCEPTOR COMPLEX

The K-15/M System (К-15/М Системы) was born out of USSR (Union of Soviet Socialist Republics – Soviet Union) research, conducted in the late 1940's through 1959, into the potential fielding of an 'automated interception system' to counter the threat of NATO (North Atlantic Treaty Organisation) intercontinental range bomber aircraft armed with atomic weapons (Laspace). The system incorporated the OKB-301 (OKB S.A. Lavochkin) La-250/A Anaconda supersonic aircraft equipped with an Institute 17 of the MAI (Ministry of Aviation Industry) K-15/M radar complex and armed with OKB-301 275, 277 or 279 air to air missiles. OKB301 had, following experience with a plethora of piston engine fighter aircraft – LaGG-1, LaGG-2, La-5/7/9/11 and a number of mixed power variants – flown its first jet powered fighter aircraft development, the La-150, in early September 1946, some five months after the maiden flights of the Yakovlev Yak-15 and Mikoyan MiG-9 turbojet powered day fighter aircraft. The La-150 was followed by the La-152, La-156, La-160, La-174TK, La-168 and the La-174/174d. The latter was effectively the prototype of the La-15 day fighter/interceptor design that entered series production. The La-15, which flew in 1948, was followed by the La-176 (the first Soviet aircraft to attain supersonic speed – achieved on 26 December 1948 (pilot, O. Sokolovsky)), La-180UTI and the La-190 day fighter developments before the bureau's attention turned to day/night all-weather radar equipped interceptors, Mikoyan and later Sukhoi having established dominant positions in the tactical fighter design/production for the Soviet air forces.

In the late 1940's, the performance of collective in service bomber aircraft, both tactical and strategic, was not much in advance of such aircraft at the end of World War II in 1945. The British Royal Air Force was operating the Avro Lincoln four piston engine bomber, a late war development of the Avro Lancaster heavy bomber – both designs considered obsolete in the second half of the 1940's. The United States operated the Boeing B-29/50 series four piston engine heavy bombers, which, although having superior performance in speed and altitude compared to the British

Lincoln, was still very vulnerable to attack by the first generation jet fighters entering service in the Soviet Union – MiG-9, Yak-15/23, MiG-15 and La-15. The Convair B-36 was larger than the wartime bombers, with better performance in regards to speed and altitude. However, it was still considered vulnerable in the face of modern air defence fighters, and more so for the planned long-range guided missile armed interceptor that it was hoped to introduce to Soviet service from the mid-1950's. It was with the jet powered bomber developments that the gap in speed performance between bomber and defensive fighter aircraft closed – the North American B-45 (US) and English Electric Canberra (British) equipping tactical units, while the Boeing B-47 six turbojet engine bomber entered widespread service with US United States SAC (Strategic Air Command). By the time the K-15 development was underway the US was preparing the Boeing B-52 eight turbojet engine strategic bomber for service whilst the trio of British 'V' bombers – Vickers Valiant, Avro Vulcan and Handley Page Victor – were being developed for service from the second half of the 1950's.

The MiG-15, the prototype of which conducted its maiden flight on 30 December 1947, ensured Soviet parity with NATO in day fighter aircraft development. RAC

Piston engine bombers in the class of the Avro Lincoln would have been employed on bombing profiles that would have crossed central frontal areas where they would have been countered by frontal tactical fighter aircraft. This would ring true for American bombers in the class of the B-29/50A, which would operate at speeds of 357 mph/385 mph (at 25,000 ft.) and ceilings of 33,600 ft./37,000 ft. (NMUSAF). The vulnerability of such designs to the first generation Soviet jet powered fighters was aptly demonstrated on a number of occasions with the interception and shooting down a number of US RB-29/RB-50 reconnaissance aircraft, which the USSR deemed had violated its airspace. A British Avro Lincoln was shot down by a MiG-15 after it apparently strayed from the Berlin air corridor in 1952 and MiG-15's caused considerable casualties among American B-29 bombers during the Korean War of 1950-1953 (Harkins 2013 & Harkins, 2018).

Top: Gun camera footage from a Soviet flown MiG-15 fighter attacking a formation of USAF B-29 bombers over North Korea c.1951-1953. Above: Convair B-36D ten engine intercontinental bomber. NMUSAF

The introduction of the six piston engine Convair B-36 was a large stride forward in the United States ability to strike targets in the Soviet Union with nuclear weapons. In its earliest operational guise the B-36 had true intercontinental range and a higher operating speed by comparison to the B-29. Range for the B-36B, declared operational with the 7th Bomb Group at Carswell AFB, Texas, in 1948, was 8,175 miles (~13156 km) with a 10,000 lb. (~4536 kg) bomb load. Maximum speed was 381 mph and service ceiling extended to 42,500 ft. (~12954 kg). The B-36D added four turbojet engines to the six piston engine power plant. This increased maximum speed to 406 mph (~653 km/h) at 36,000 ft. (~10973 m) with a 42,200 ft. (~12863 m) service ceiling. Total round trip range was 7,500 miles (~12070 km) with a 10,000 lb. bomb load. The ten engine B-36F extended speed to 417 mph (~671 km/h). Combat radius was 3,200 miles (~5150 km) with a 10,000 lb. bomb load and service ceiling was 44,000 ft. (~13411 m). The B-36H maximum speed was 416 mph, combat radius with a 10,000 lb. bomb load, 3,200 miles and service ceiling was 44,000 ft. The RB-36D extended range to around 10,000 miles (~16093 km). Maximum speed was 408 mph (~657 km/h) and service ceiling extended to 50,000 ft. (~15240 km). These values remained valid for the RB-36E. The RB-36F retained the 10,000 mile range, maximum speed was 417 mph and service ceiling was above 50,000 ft. The RB-36H had a maximum speed of 420 mph (~676 km/h) and, whilst service ceiling remained above 50,000 ft., range dropped to 8,000 miles (~12875 km/h) (NMUSAF).

USAF Boeing B-47E-50-LM serial number 52-3363. NMUSAF

It would be to avoid historical-technical fact to deny that the B-36 variants would have been extremely vulnerable to Soviet defensive capabilities from the late 1940's. The jet powered B-47 offered increased survivability by comparison to the B-36, due principally to its higher operating speed and altitude, but it lacked the range and load carrying capability of the larger Convair aircraft. The first B-47A service test aircraft conducted its maiden flight in spring 1950 and the first B-47B service variant conducted its maiden flight on 26 April 1952. Powered by six GE J47-GE-24 axial flow turbojets, maximum speed was 630 mph (~1014 km/h) at sea level and 560 mph (~901 km/h) at 35,000 ft. (~10668 m). Operational range with a 10,000 lb. bomb load was 3,870 miles (~6228 km), almost half that of the B-36D. Service ceiling was 45,000 ft. (~13715 m), only slightly higher that of the B-36D/F/H bomber variants. Maximum speed of the B-47E, which conducted its maiden flight on 30 Jan 1953, was 610 mph (~982 km), cruise speed 590 mph (~950 km) and range was 3,500 miles (~5633 km) (NMUSAF). The poor range of the B-47 made it less than ideal for attacks on Russian territory from the direction of the Arctic. The standard tactic was forward deploying such aircraft to European NATO countries for attack profiles that would have been countered by frontal aviation fighters and air defence fighters.

The B-47's range shortfalls would be overcome with the B-52 Stratofortress, which could fly high subsonic speed, high altitude mission profiles against targets in the Soviet Union, primarily operating over Arctic region to penetrate the Soviet Union's vast Northern boundaries. It was this theatre that the K-15/M System was intended to operate in to provide an airborne barrier armed with guided missiles that would destroy incoming nuclear armed strategic bombers attempting to penetrate the Soviet Union's northern and eastern boundaries.

USAF Boeing B-52B eight turbojet strategic bomber. NMUSAF

The first XB-52 to fly was the second prototype, which conducted its maiden flight on 15 April 1952. The B-52A conducted its maiden flight in 1954. The first serial production variant was the B-52B, which conducted its maiden flight on 25 January 1955. This variant had a maximum speed of 630 mph (~1014 km) at (20,000 ft. (~6096 m), a service ceiling of 47,000 ft. (~14326 m) and a combat radius of 3,600 miles (~5794 km) without in-flight refuelling, allowing attacks on the Soviet Union over northern routes across the Arctic. This remained the case for the major Stratofortress bomber variants – B-52F/E/D/G/H – the latter variant having a maximum speed of 650 mph (~1046 km/h) (Boeing & NMUSAF).

While the K-16 System was developed to counter large scale attacks by B-36/B-52 class bombers, it was clear that it could have to counter the supersonic capable Convair B-58, the prototype of which conducted its maiden flight in 1956 (entered service in early 1960's). This design would possess considerably higher performance characteristics than its subsonic forebears, with a final cruise altitude on a maximum range mission of 50159 ft. (~15288 m). Maximum combat radius was in the order of 4,226 miles (~6901 kg) with a 6,230 lb. (~2926 kg) payload. Maximum speed at a service ceiling of 58,300 ft. (~17770 m) was 1147 knots (~2124 km/h) (SAC B/RB-58A, 1959). While operating at maximum speed over the combat zone (penetrating Soviet airspace), the B-58A would have proved a difficult target for an interceptor in the class of the K-15/M System. The B-58A speed outside the target zone, which would have included the approach to the Soviet border regions – the areas that interception by the K-15 System would have been affected, would have been in the region of 539 knots (998 km), well within the standard interception parameters for the K-15/M System.

Convair B-58-15-CF supersonic strategic bomber. The supersonic speed capability increased the penetration capability of the Strategic Air Command – this not being among the target types the original K-15 System was have had to counter. NMUSAF

The G-300 carrier platform was developed from the Tupolev Tu-4K(KS) missile carrier developed from the Tu-4 conventional bomber (above). The Tu-4K proved the ability of the Tu-4 design to successfully launch large missiles from underwing stations (production of the KS-1 air to surface missile commenced in 1951), paving the way for flight tests of the G-310 with the 211 and 210 air to air missiles. Tupolev

The early Soviet attempts at developing a viable long-range radar guided interceptor capability for the air defence forces of the Soviet Union were unorthodox. As a sideline to the development of the S-25 SAM (Surface to Air Missile) complex that would utilise the B-300 missile, the OKB-301 G-300 missile was developed from the B-300 as a guided air to air missile to arm the G-310 (Tupolev Tu-4 development) four piston engine (derived from the Boeing B-29) launch platform. The Tu-4 had conducted its maiden flight in 1947 (pilot, N. Rybko) and became operational as a long range conventional bomber with Long Range Aviation of the Soviet Union in 1949. The entry of the Soviet Union as a nuclear power, in 1949, paved the way for the Tu-4A, a batch of ten Tu-4's adapted to operate with the first Soviet Atomic bomb, the RDS-1 (Tupolev).

The large numbers of Tu-4's flooding Soviet air forces in several roles allowed allocation of the type as a test-bed launch platform for the G-300 long-range all-weather interceptor concept. The G-310 launch vehicle and the G-300 missile were collectively referred to as the Complex G-300, the Tu-4 derivative being modelled on the Tu-4K(KS) missile carrier, 50 of which were procured for Long Range Aviation, to be armed with the KS-1 air to surface missile (Laspace & Tupolev). The rational for the Complex G-300 was to combine the capability of long-range radar stations (normally located at surface level) with that of an interceptor aircraft within a single platform. The radar stations installed on the aircraft consisted of four Typhoon D-500 stations, which were credited with a detection range of 80-100 km (Laspace). The large size aircraft required to carry the radar stations facilitated the long-range of the system as the Tu-4 could fly farther and for longer than a tactical combat size aircraft.

The G-310 launch platform for the Complex G-300 was derived from the Tu-4K series missile carrier. The photograph (top), despite having the G-300 designation superimposed, appears to show a Tu-4K(KS) missile carrier adaption of the Tu-4 bomber armed with KS-1 air to surface anti-ship missiles on the underwing stations. The 210 guided missile intended for the Complex G-300 was derived from the ZUR 205 SAM (above). Laspace

Lavochkin was authorised to enter full-scale development of the Concept G-300 by a decree of the Soviet government dated 23 September 1950. Development of the

G-300 air to air guided missiles to be carried by the G-310 was authorised in 1951. OKB-301 developed two separate variants of the G-300 missile, one carrying the factory index 211 and the other carrying the factory index 210. The latter was developed as a smaller variant of the ZUR 205 SAM. The changes included a reduction in diameter from the 650 mm of the ZUR 205 to 530 mm in the 210 missile. Length was reduced from 11.3 m (ZUR 205) to 8.3 m (210). The completed 210 design had a launch mass of 1000 kg. The 211, which was a modification of the 210, was designed with an aerodynamic layout that incorporated what was known as the 'duck 2' wing type, but better described as an 'X' planform. Like the 210, the 211 missile was powered by a single-chamber LPRE (Liquid Propellant Rocket Engine) featuring 'two degrees of control' (Laspace). Fuel was supplied to the rocket engine with the aid of an air pressure accumulator. The missiles were designed with the capability to engage a diversity of high speed target types at altitudes up to 20 km. Four missiles could be carried by the G-310 launch platform – two under each wing. The missiles would be launched from the G-310 wing stations by the use of '2 powder accelerators' that were 'located on the sides of the rocket [missile] between the wing consoles' – both missile variants were armed with a 100 kg warhead sufficient to destroy large multi-engine bomber aircraft (Laspace).

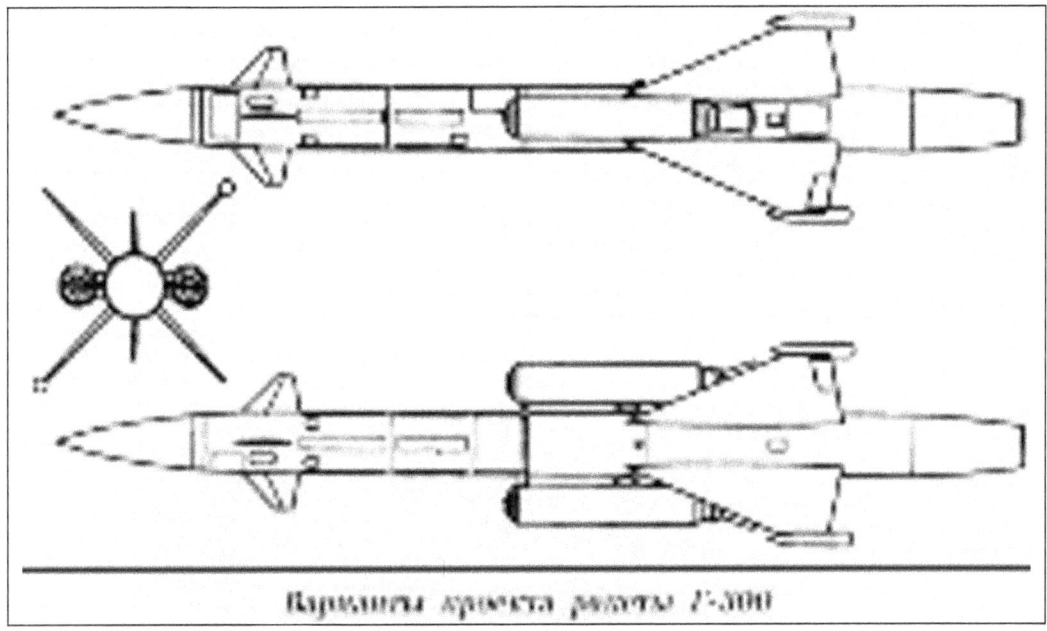

The large missiles of the 211/210 types developed for the Complex G-300 would be carried in a similar manner. Laspace

The G-310 airborne launch vehicle was ready for flight testing to commence by early summer 1952, the maiden flight being conducted in May that year. During the course of May and June 1952 a total of 10 flights were conducted with the aircraft carrying inert 211/210 missiles. Ground test launches of the 211 missile were conducted from late 1952, but development of this weapon was suspended by a decree of the Soviet government (No. 2837-1200) dated 20 November 1953, and, on 16 August the following year, work was completely cancelled on the entire Complex G-300. This was in the context of progression of work for the 275 air to air guided missiles for carriage by an all-weather interceptor that would be developed into the K-15 System (Laspace).

The maturation of powerful airborne radar complexes for carriage in interceptor size aircraft was one of the driving forces behind the research that would lead to the K-15 System. The Soviet Union had been trailed its western allies and German opponents in development of radar systems during World War II. The first Soviet operational radar was the EN 2, which was employed operationally on 21 September 1941, against German bomber aircraft attacking Soviet Baltic Fleet warships. The Redoubt-3 of the 72nd Battalion detected the airborne targets at a distance of 200 km (MODRF). V. Tikhomirov had been at the forefront of Soviet airborne radar developments since involvement in the first domestic Soviet airborne radar, the Gneis-2, which was fitted to Petlyakov Pe-2 and Pe-3 frontal bombers in the latter part of World War II, having entered service in 1943. In excess of 230 aircraft had been equipped with Gneiss-2 by the end of 1944 (MODRF).

During the Gneis-2 developed, Tikhomirov was with NII-20 (the modern day All-Russia Scientific Research Institute of Radiotechics). With the war over in 1945, airborne radar development for Soviet combat aircraft was centred on NII-17 (modern day JSC Concern Vega), to which Tikhomirov was moved. A splinter branch of NII-17 formed at the M.M. Gromov Flight Research Institute at Zhukovsky in 1955, with 379 personnel transferred from NII-17. This embryonic gathering would directly lead to the modern day JSC 'Research Institute for Instrument Engineering, V.V. Tikhomirov (NIIP V. Tikhomirov).

The Lavochkin La-200, which conducted its maiden flight on 16 September 1949, was developed as a cannon armed fighter/interceptor, employing a 'Tory-A' radar complex to detect and home on the target. Laspace

While the Soviet Union continued research & development programs pushing toward achieving the goal of introducing an all-weather long-range interception capability – a high performance aircraft armed with long-range guided missiles capable of intercepting American long-range bombers armed with nuclear weapons that posed a considerable threat to the Soviet homeland – the less ambitious requirement of fielding a cannon/unguided rocket armed all-weather fighter capability was far more readily achieved. Lavochkin continued design studies that resulted in the La-200, a jet powered fighter/interceptor prototype that conducted its maiden flight on 16 September 1949. The La-200, which was designed for day/night operations in adverse weather conditions at medium and high altitudes, was powered by two VK-1 turbojet engines. The engine were arranged in tandem, the fore unit installed at an inclined angle of 10° to the aircraft axis with the aft unit, housed in the tail section, effectively standing on the aircraft axis, both being fed air form a nose mounted air intake. To achieve interception of the target the La-200 was to be equipped with a 'Tory-A' radar complex, housed in the intake central body. The radar operated in the centimeter range for target detection and calculating a firing solution to the target, which would be destroyed by the cannon armament – three H-37 37 mm cannon, two on the starboard side lower bow of the aircraft and one on the port side. The two-crew (pilot and systems operator) were seated side by side in a cockpit that incorporated armour protection and a single instrument panel (Laspace).

A La-200 prototype was built and prepared for its maiden flight, which, as noted above, was conducted on 16 September 1949 (crew, S.F. Mashkovsky and A.F. Kosarev). State tests were successfully completed in 1950. However, a redesign was authorised to address inadequacies in the original design, this concerning the forward fuselage section and incorporation of a new 'Korshun' radar complex, which superseded the 'Tory-A'. Further tests continued with the aircraft in 1951, leading to a recommendation to move to serial production. However, changing operational requirements, including the need for increased range, led to the programs cancellation before serial production was authorised (Laspace).

Model of the Yak-25 exhibited in the Yakovlev museum. Yakovlev

Yakovlev design bureau was also involved in development work intended to arrive at a viable all-weather day/night cannon armed interceptor. This design emerged as the Yak-25 (chief engineer, M. Leonov, designer, A. Yakovlev OKB), which flew on 19 June 1952. The Yak-25 was powered by 2 x RD-5A turbojet engines, each rated at 2000 kgf (~19.6 kN). Take-off weight was put at 9220 kg (~20,326 lb.), maximum speed, 1090 km/h (~677 mph), range, 2010 km (~1248 miles) and ceiling, 13900 m (~45,603 ft.). The design was equipped with a nose mounted radar complex and armed with 2 x H-37 37 mm cannon and unguided rockets (Yakovlev).

Lavochkin was still in the race to field an all-weather interceptor in-line with a new set of operational requirements, which had been issued in August 1951. In November that year, OKB-301 embarked upon a complete redesign of the La-200, which would now be equipped with an improved Sokol radar complex, and powered by VK-1A engines. The basic mission remained the same, the interception of airborne targets at medium and high altitudes, but the range requirement for the new design, designated La-200B, was increased to 2500 km. Once an interception had been effected then the target would be destroyed by the cannon armament – the three H-37 arrangement, carried over from the La-200 (Laspace).

Manufacturer's flight testing, which commenced on 3 July 1952, was completed on 10 September that year. The aircraft was flown by pilots Ya.I. Vernikov, V.N. Komarov, K.B. Makarov and A.F. Kosarev. The initial flight tests were conducted with a mock-up of the Sokol radar complex installed. However, in line with an MAI order, the La-200B was equipped with a functional Sokol radar complex in January 1953, flight testing in this configuration commencing that month (Laspace).

The La-200B, developed from the La-200 to meet a new set of operational requirements, commenced flight testing on 3 July 1952. Laspace

The La-200B was not selected to proceed to serial production, the Yak-25 going on to become the first operational all-weather/day/night interceptor in Soviet service – 483 built in the period 1954-1957 (Yakovlev). Plant No.339 (Phazotron – the modern day JSC Fazotron-NIIR) delivered series production 'Falcon' radar systems for the Yak-25 from 1955 (Fazotron-NIIR). The Yak-25 was further developed as the Yak-25PB (RV) reconnaissance aircraft. The prototype flew in 1959 and 155 aircraft were built in the period 1961-1965. The Yak-25 was again further developed to improve its interceptor capability. This effort would lead to the Yak-27 development powered by 2 x RD-9F turbojet engines, each rated at 3850 kgf (~37.3 kN)). Production of the Yak-27, the prototype of which conducted its maiden flight in 1956, extended to 180 aircraft built between 1959 and 1962. The single crew Yak-27 could fly at a speed of 1270 km/h (~789 mph), had a range of 1300 km (~807 miles) and a ceiling of 16300 m (~53477 ft.). Armament consisted of a single 23 mm cannon and TRS-85, S-190 unguided air to air rockets (Yakovlev & Laspace).

Artist rendering of the K-15M System of the late 1950's. Laspace

The La-200B, which had conducted 109 flights by the time of its cancellation, had fallen by the wayside not only because of the decision to put the Yak-25 into serial production, but also the fact that design studies had commenced at OKB-301 for a more advanced all-weather/day/night interceptor. This would emerge as the La-250 designed to meet a new set of operational requirements. The La-250 had emerged from an April 1953 proposal by Lavochkin and the head of Institute-17, V.V. Tikhomirov (radar), for a high performance – supersonic – day/night all-weather interceptor, equipped with a high power generating radar complex. The aircraft and radar were to be designed around a weapon system concept that included incorporation of long-range guided air to air missiles to facilitate a system of automated interception of a target – primarily determined to be large strategic bombers of the B-36 or B-52 types. This concept, referred to as the K-15 System, effectively took the place of the earlier studies that had spawned the now cancelled Complex G-300.

Although the Yak-25 and Yak-27 provided much needed all-weather day/night airborne interception capability for the Soviet air defence forces, these designs fell far short of the advanced capability being developed with the K-15 System. Development work officially commenced on the K-15 System – this would eventually cover the La-250 aircraft, the K-15 radar complex and the 275 guided missile armament as a single weapon system concept – by order of Soviet government, resolution No. 2837-1200 of 20 November 1953 (Laspace).

The K-15 System was designed to intercept targets flying at high speeds (in excess of Mach 1) – up to 1200 km/h (~745 mph) – at altitudes up to 20 km (~12 miles) (Laspace). The number 15 in the K-15 System designation referred to the planned range for the guided missile armament – 15 km (Laspace) – which, in the mid-1950's, was a quantum leap over the within gun range interception capability of then current Soviet fighter aircraft and interceptors. This was also considerably in advance of the armament specified for the US MX-1554 interceptor (this program spawned the Convair F-102 interceptor, which served US ADC (Air Defence Command) and foreign air forces, armed with GAR-1 (later AIM-4 Falcon) air to air missile, which had an effective range of (~1524-7620 m (5,000-25,000 ft.) at altitudes up to ~18288 m (60,000 ft.) (Harkins, 2019 & CS GAR-1, 1954).

OKB-301 took on the task of developing the La-250 aircraft and the 275 guided missile armament, whilst Institute-17 took on the task of development of the K-15 radar complex. The La-250 was to be powered by two VRD (Klimov) VK-9 engines, each of which developed a thrust of 12000 kg (26,455 lb.) when afterburner was applied (Laspace & MODRF).

The La-250 design took on a new aerodynamic configuration for a Soviet aircraft. The designer description details an aircraft designed with 'a free-bearing mid-plane with a triangular [delta] wing of a large sweep [57° sweepback angle at the leading edge], an arrow-shaped tail and a three-wheeled [tricycle] chassis [undercarriage] that retracts into the fuselage' (Laspace). The undercarriage actually consisted of four wheels – two single wheel main units and a twin wheel nose unit – the designer description referring to three undercarriage units. The tailed delta (thin wing) layout featured 'a low-lying all-turn [all-moving] stabilizer [tail planes]' (Laspace) and a single vertical tail fin. The flight control system consisted of twin hydraulic systems powering double chamber irreversible hydraulic actuators, driving the various control surfaces, which included wing trailing-edge flaps, the all moving tail planes and a conventional single piece hinged rudder on the trailing-edge of the single vertical tail unit. The flight control system would also have actuated the release for the two 275 guided air to air missiles, which would have been carried semi-recessed in tandem bays on the fuselage underside. An anti-icing system was incorporated to meet the demands of flying at high altitudes. The two fuselage mounted engines were fed air through 'supersonic air intakes' laterally mounted with inlet areas adjacent to the cockpit section (Laspace). Fuel tankage was ~8,000 kg, a significant portion of the standard take-off of weight of 25000 kg (just under 28 tons). The two crew – pilot and weapons system operator (referred to simply as operator in Soviet parlance) – were seated on ejection seats in tandem within an unarmoured cockpit section

(Laspace). The target detection and fire control system – the K-15 complex – was designed to be in advance of the simple detection and ranging units and early interception units in service in the early to mid-1950's, such as the Izumrud-2 equipping the MiG-17PFU (NIIP V. Tikhomirov). The new radar complex would have to be capable of calculating a launch solution and guiding the large beam-riding or SARH (Semi-Active Radar Homing) missile armament to the target area. In this regard, the target engagement sequence, including weapon launch, would no longer be undertaken by the crew, but conducted automatically by the automatic control system (Laspace).

The first generation radar complex to bestow a significant adverse weather/night capability on Soviet tactical fighters, included the V. Tikhomirov, Institute 17, Izumrud-2, which equipped the MiG-17PFU from the early 1950's. NIIP V. Tikhomirov

The La-250A (centre of photo) featured a single vertical tail unit incorporating a single piece hinged rudder on the trailing-edge. MODRF

There were many problems encountered during development of the La-250, not least of which was considerable delays with development of the VK-9 (modern day Klimov) power plant. The engine problems were so serious that the decision was taken to substitute the VK-9 with the considerably less powerful AL-7F-1 (modern day NPO Saturn) turbojet engine derived from the AL-7F powering the Sukhoi Su-7 frontal attack fighter. The AL-7F-1 was rated at 8950 kgf (90. 2 kN). The need to substitute the VK-9 with the AL-7F-1, which was overall smaller compared to the VK-9, coincided with a wider 1955 overhaul of the K-15 System, which would lead to a redesigned aircraft designated La-250A. Besides the new engines, the La-250A was to be equipped with the updated, more capable, K-15M radar complex and redesigned, lighter weight, 275A (conventional warhead) air to air guided missiles. At a later date two new radar guided missile developments with semi-active radar homing heads – the 277 (conventional warhead) and the 279 (nuclear warhead) – were specified for the K-15 System. These would be employed in addition to, rather than as replacements for, the 275A missile (Laspace). The nuclear armed 279 warhead would vastly increase kill probability over that of the conventional armed 277 and 275A weapons, extending the range of target performance that could be engaged to those beyond the 1200 km/h.

In effect, there were two distinct, but related variants of the K-15 System. 1. The K-15 System, consisting of the La-250 powered by two VK-9 engines, equipped with the K-15 radar complex and armed with the 275 missile, which was not brought to fruition. 2. The K-15M System, consisting of the La-250A aircraft, 275A (factory index 278), 279 and 277 air to air missiles and the K-15M radar complex (Laspace). As construction of the prototype La-250 was advanced at the time of the redesign decision, this aircraft was completed with modifications to allow it to contribute to the overall K-15M System development effort under the power of two AL-31F-1's. The La-250, designated 250-I, was competed in early summer 1956 (pilot, A.G. Kochtkov) and conducted its maiden flight on 16 July that year (Laspace).

The first La-250A, 250A-I, was extensively damaged in a landing accident on its sixth flight in November 1957.

Aircraft basic characteristics included a length of 24.6 m; height, 7.26 m; wingspan, 13.9 m; wing area, 80 m²; empty weight, 15 tons and take-off weight, ~28 tons. The La-250A was slightly reduced in overall size/mass compared to the La-250. Among the most notable external differences between the two variants was in the arrangement of the missile armament carriage – the two missiles now being suspended under the wings of the La-250A rather than the semi-recessed fuselage underside arrangement of the La-250 (Laspace).

Development of the 275 missile had commenced at OKB-301 in 1954, the development effort switching to the 'radio-controlled', beam riding 275A, which was lighter than the 275 design, following year (Laspace). The requirement for the reduced weight 275A missile was, in part, fueled by the reduced power available through the switch to the AL-7F-1 engine. The arrangement adopted for the 275A, which was powered by a single chamber, two-stage LPRE located in the rear of the missile body, consisted of '4 wings and 4 rudders' – cruciform configuration – which were positioned 'in the horizontal and vertical planes' (Laspace). Initial guidance to the general target area would still be conducted under ground control, the K-15M System to be integrated into the overall air defence system that would utilise a number of different surface (and later airborne) radar types available to the Soviet Union. The onboard K-15M radar complex would then acquire the target, commencing the terminal phase of the target engagement. The profile for the 275A missile employment called for the weapon to be launched at altitudes between 5 and 14 km with the La-250A launch platform flying at speeds ranging between 1400 and 1540 km/h (Laspace). The control system for the 275A missile was based on the concept of 'paralleled approach', the operator in the La-250A then positioning the aircraft in the optimum position for the missile to engage the target with the greatest chance of success. The terminal phase of the interception was completely controlled by the aircraft autopilot/automatic control system – the first such system developed in the Soviet Union – which received direct data inputs form the onboard airborne calculating device. The target was destroyed or disabled by the 125-140 kg fragmentation warhead located behind the guidance system (Laspace). As development of the K-15M System matured, two new air to air guided missile were added to the planned armoury of the K-15M System as noted above – the 277 (armed with a conventional warhead) and the 279 (armed with a nuclear warhead) (Laspace). Addition of these new weapons would considerably increasing the ability for the design to destroy intercontinental bombers and cruise missiles on attack profiles against the Soviet Union's vast northern or eastern regions.

Three-quarters frontal aspect view of La-250A, Red 03, demonstrating the downward inclination of the new nose design. Laspace

The first La-250A prototype, designated 250A-I, was completed in early 1957 and entered a series of ground testing of systems. In April 1957, the aircraft entered intensive preparation for its maiden flight, which was conducted on 12 July that year (pilot, A.G. Kochtkov) (Laspace). Among the concerns that emerged from early flight tests was the poor forward view afforded the pilot on the approach and landing, attributed, in part, to the designs rather elongated nose section. This flaw was firmly brought to the fore when the aircraft was damaged when landing in foggy conditions at the end of the sixth flight (Laspace), apparently on 28 November 1957.

Experience gained with the 250A-I resulted in the second La-250A, 250A-II, being built with a slightly dropped nose section – apparently a downward angle of 6° to the horizontal plane. The second development aircraft was completed in early 1958 and entered ground testing in May that year in preparation for its maiden flight, which was conducted on 30 July 1958 (pilot, A.P. Bogorodsky). This aircraft conducted a total of 16 flights. The first two La-250 aircraft, 250A-I and 250A-II, were tasked with proving the basic flight characteristics of the La-250A design. Two more La-250A aircraft, 250A-III and 250A-IV, were advanced in construction by late 1958. These aircraft would be tasked with proving the K-15M radar complex and the missile armament, with a series of planned missile launches leading up to demonstration of the automated interception capability. By this time it had become clear that aircraft platforms would be the secondary target set intended for interception with the K-15M System. The design emphasis of the system had moved toward the primary interception of guided missile complexes cruising at speeds up to 1200 km/h at altitudes up to 20000 m – the North American AGM-28 Hound Dog (program initiated in August 1957 (AGM-28A CS, 1972) as armament for the American B-52 bomber) flew much of its mission profile within the engagement parameters of the K-15M System. As noted above, development of the 277 and 279 missiles were intended to increase lethality against targets in the AGM-28 class, the performance of which was unknown when the K-15M System was under development.

Top and above: In 1959, Lavochkin undertook a flight test phase on La-250A code 02, configured with two aerodynamic models of the 275A air to air guided missile on the underwing stations.

The La-250A was flown with aerodynamic models of the 275A missile during 1959 (Laspace). There was no missile test launch from an La-250A with operable

275A missiles, but the complex underwent an extensive ground test program that included a number of surface launches, conducted using missiles configured with piston accelerators launched from a ground launch vehicle. The missiles were controlled from a purpose built ground based radar/control complex, which controlled the missile flight and guided the missile to the target area (Laspace). Development of the 277 and 279 missile complexes did not reach the flight test or ground launch phases prior to their respective cancellation.

La-250A specification – data furnished by Laspace and Central Museum of the Aerospace Force – Monino

Chief designer: M. Baranovski
Test pilot, maiden flight: A. Kochtkov
Engines: 2 x AL-7F-1 turbojet
Engine thrust: 8950 kgf (90. 2 kN) each
Take-off weight: 25000 kg
Range: 2000 km
Maximum speed: 2000 km/h
Ceiling: 18000 m
Armament: 275, 277 or 279 (nuclear warhead) guided air to air missiles
Crew: 2

La-250/A Test Aircraft

Variant	Maiden Flight	Pilot
La-250 static test example	N/A	N/A
La-250-I	16 July 1956	A.G. Kochtkov
La-250A-I	12 July 1957	A.G. Kochtkov
La-250A-II	30 July 1958	A.P. Bogorodsky
La-250A-III	N/A	N/A
La-250A-IV	N/A	N/A

As the K-15/M System was being developed as a long-range system for the interception of strategic attack targets attempting to penetrate the Soviet Union's northern and eastern regions, development of a shorter range system was carried out simultaneously for operations in defence of the Soviet Union's western (including eastern European satellite states) and southern regions. This emerged as the Sukhoi T-3 (Su-9) equipped with the K-51 radar complex, intended for the frontal interception role (Sukhoi) – interception of airborne targets in regions expected to be the scene of ground offensive/defensive operations. The T-3 development aircraft had conducted its maiden flight on 26 May 1956 (pilot, V.N. Makhalin) (Sukhoi), around a month and a half ahead of the La-250-I maiden flight. The decision was taken to launch serial production of the T-3 on 24 August 1956 and the Su-9 (T-43-1) conducted its maiden flight on 10 October 1957. The first serial production Su-9 conducted its maiden flight at Plant Number 153 on 3 May 1958 (pilot, V.N. Pronyakin) and the type entered service with a Soviet air defence regiment on 12 May 1959 (Sukhoi). The Su-9 was designed to intercept a wider set of targets compared to the K-15 System – bomber size down to tactical combat size fighter, ground attack, tactical reconnaissance and light bomber aircraft – expected to be encountered over an active ground war zone. For this mission it required higher performance in areas such as maximum operating speed and altitude – the Su-9 demonstrated its high operating altitude/high speed attributes when it achieved an altitude of 21500 m and a speed of 2200 km/h on 30 October and 02 November 1956 respectively (Sukhoi). The Su-9 would be possessed of shorter range by comparison to the K-15/M System as the regions to be covered were considerably less in area and remoteness than that required for the K-15/M System operations over the vast expenses of the Russian Soviet Republic's northern arctic coastline and the Far East regions. The automated interception capability of the K-15/M System was considerably more capable than the K-51 System developed for the Su-9.

Top: The Su-9 was developed as a supersonic interceptor for operations covering the Soviet Union's less remote areas, particularly in the western, southern and south eastern regions. Above: The Sukhoi P-1 two-seat interceptor prototype conducted its maiden flight on 9 July 1957. Sukhoi

Another Sukhoi design, the P-1 two-seat interceptor development, which conducted its maiden flight on 9 July 1957 (pilot, N.I. Korovushkin), may be considered a rival in the competition that spawned the K-15M System and ultimately the Tupolev Tu-128. Although the P-1 underwent factory flight tests during the course of 1957-1958, the program was cancelled due to problems procuring suitable engines (Sukhoi). The following year, 1959, the K-15M System was cancelled by OKB-301, ostensibly to free up work capacity for other projects in the wake of Tupolev being selected to go forward with a long-range all-weather missile armed interception system referred to as the 'Heavy Interception System', un-flown at the time of the K-15M System cancellation (Laspace).

The decision to cancel the K-15M System can be considered a combination of technical and political. The unavailability of the VK-9 engine and subsequent reliance on the AL-7F-1 turbojet had the drawback of lower overall operating performance. Reported performance values for the flight test aircraft included a speed of 1080 km/h and a ceiling in the order of 13.3 km. While there has been criticism that this was overly disappointing as it failed to reach the design performance values, it should be noted that the aircraft flown were not configured for full envelope expansion flight testing. One area of testing that had not commenced was maximum speed and ceiling trials, two important aspects for the aircrafts operational role to intercept high speed targets flying at altitudes in excess of 20000 m. What is clear is that the intended final performance of the K-15M System was in, for the most part, in excess of that which would emerge from the program that replaced it in the quest to field an all-weather/long range interceptor to defend the Soviet Union's northern and eastern regions – the Tupolev Tu-128 (NATO reporting name 'Fiddler'). This program, an evolution of the Tu-28-80, would be developed for more or less the same role as the smaller K-15M System.

The Tupolev 98 was developed as a supersonic frontal bomber. Experience gained on the '98', which did not proceed to serial production, facilitated Tupolev's development of the Tu-28-80, which evolved into the Tu-128 long-range interceptor. Tupolev

The program that spawned the Tu-128 had its origins in a multi-design bureau competition to develop a medium/large aircraft capable of supersonic speeds. This effort splintered into three prongs to develop a supersonic replacement for the subsonic Ilyushin Il-28 twin-jet frontal bomber, a longer range bomber to replace the subsonic Tupolev Tu-16 long-range jet powered bomber and an intercontinental range aircraft to replace the subsonic Tupolev Tu-95 four turboprop bomber/missile carrier and the subsonic four turbojet powered Myasishchev M-4 bomber. To meet the first requirement, Tupolev developed the Tupolev 98. Although this design was not carried through to serial production, the supersonic speed tests results put Tupolev in a position to develop the design further to field a long-range interceptor competitor to the K-15M System in the shape of the Tu-28-80, which evolved into the Tu-128 developed through the first half of the 1960's (Tupolev).

Like the La-250A, the Tu-128 was a two crew aircraft. It was powered by two AL-7F2 turbojet engines, which, at a rating of 10100 kg (99 kN) each, were notably more powerful than the AL-7F-1 engines powering the La-250A. However, the additional power of the engines was offset by the heavier weight of the Tu-128 – the Tu-128 weighed in at 43000 kg, 15000 kg heavier than the 28000 kg of the La-250A. Range of the Tu-128, at 2565 km, was in excess of 500 km more than that planned for the La-250A, but maximum design speed, 1665 km/h, and ceiling, 15600 km, were inferior to that planned for the Lavochkin aircraft – maximum speed, 2000 km/h and ceiling, 18000 m respectively. Combat persistence of the Tupolev aircraft, which could carry four large R-4 (NATO reporting index and name AA-5 'Ash') guided air to air missiles, was superior to that of the La-250A, which had a standard armament of two large missiles – 275A or 277 (conventional warhead) or 279 (nuclear warhead) – the Tu-128 being armed only with missiles with conventional warheads (Laspace & Tupolev). The Tu-128 was equipped with a 'Smerch' radar complex, development of which had commenced at what had become OKB-339 (formerly Plant No.339) in 1958 (Fazotron-NIIR). This complex, which continued development through to 1965, would eventually surpass the specified detection and acquisition range capability of the K-15M radar of the K-15M System.

Page 23-24: The Tu-128 was selected to proceed to serial production as the Soviet Union's long-range/all-weather/day/night interceptor, serving with Soviet air defence units from 1965 until the mid-1980's. MODRF/Tupolev

The Tu-128 conducted its maiden flight in 1961 (pilot, M. Kozlov) and entered operational service in 1965 (Fazotron-NIIR). Around 120 Tu-128 aircraft were built and the design served with Soviet air defence forces in several regiments, remaining in operational service until the mid-1980's (Tupolev & MODRF). In service the Tu-128 was tasked with the defence of the Soviet Union's vast northern coastline and territorial waters extending beyond, from United States strategic bombers transiting across Arctic regions to deliver a nuclear strike on Soviet territory. This would have been the role that would have been undertaken by the K-15/M System had fortune shone more favourably on the Lavochkin program.

A single La-250A of the K-15M System survives in the second decade of the twenty first century, exhibited in the Museum of the Russian Federation Aerospace Forces, Monino. MODRF

The Tu-128 displayed operational advantages and disadvantages over the K-15M System. However, its biggest advantage was political, in that Tupolev was held in high favour in regard to aircraft production in the Soviet Union. It should be considered that the Tu-128 was selected to continue to serial production due to political favour rather than a realistic service entry schedule for a technically more capable interception system. While it is historical fact that the Tu-128 was not ready for service until 1965, Laspace also contends that the Tupolev system was inferior, both technically and tactically, compared with the K-15M System (Laspace), such a hypothesis, which would be open to contestation, being impossible to prove as the Tu-128 program benefitted from technological advances in the six years between cancellation of the K-15M System and the introduction to service of the Tu-128. What is clear is that the cancellation of the K-15M program saw OKB-301 leave the field of inhabited aircraft development, the future direction of the company being directed at uninhabited aircraft, long-range missile systems and Solar System space exploration developments. A single La-250A survives in the twenty first century, this aircraft was transferred to the Soviet air forces museum at Monino, Moscow, in 1967.

GLOSSARY

ADC	Air Defence Command
B	Bomber
ft.	Feet (unit of measurement)
Il	Ilyushin
Institute 17	Institute 17 was formed on 1 March 1955 as a distinct branch of the Soviet Ministry of Aviation Industry, evolving into the present day JSC NIIP V. Tikhomirov (JSC 'Research Institute for Instrument Engineering, V.V. Tikhomirov)
kg	Kilogram
kgf	Kilogram force
km	Kilometer
km/h	Kilometers per hour
kN	Kilo newton
Knots	Nautical miles per hour (1 knot - ~1.15 mph)
La	Lavochkin
lb.	Pound (unit of weight)
m	metre
MAI	Ministry of Aviation Industry
MiG	Mikoyan
MODRF	Ministry of Defence of the Russian Federation
NMUSAF	National Museum of the United States Air Force
OKB-301	Renamed OKB S.A. Lavochkina after chief designer S.A. Lavochkin, and then changed to Scientific and Industrial Association them. S.A. Lavochkina
OKB-339	Formerly Plant No.339 – present day JSC Fazotron-NIIR
Pe	Petlyakov
RB	Reconnaissance Bomber
SAC	Strategic Air Command
SAM	Surface to Air Missile
Su	Sukhoi
Tu	Tupolev
US	United States
USAF	United States Air Force
USSR	Union of Soviet Socialist Republics (Soviet Union)
x	Times (multiplication)
Yak	Yakovlev

ABOUT THE AUTHOR

Hugh Harkins FRAS is a historian and author with an extensive research background in astro/geophysics and studies/research in the wider scientific, aeronautic, astronautic and nautical technical and historical fields. He is also involved in research in the field of Scottish history, which formed a significant element of an otherwise scientific undergraduate degree. Hugh has published in excess of sixty books; non-fiction and fiction, writing under his given name as well as utilising several pseudonyms. He has also written for several international magazines, whilst his work has been used as reference for many other projects, ranging from the aviation industry, international news corporations and film media to encyclopaedias, museum exhibits and the computer gaming industry. Hugh is a member of the Institute of Physics and is an elected Fellow of the Royal Astronomical Society. He currently resides in his native Scotland. Other titles by the author include:

Soviet Mixed Power Experimental Fighter Aircraft – Piston-Liquid Propellant Rocket Engine/Piston-Ramjet/Piston-Pulsejet & Piston-Compressor Jet Engine Designs of the 1940's
Sukhoi T-4 – The Soviet Mach 3+ Hypersonic Missile Carrier/Airborne Reconnaissance System
Orbital/Fractional Orbit Bombardment System - The Soviet Globalnaya Raketa
Counter-Space Defence Co-Orbital Satellite Fighter
Soviet/Russian Laser Weapon Development, X-2 M & B-1 KLO/A-60 Ladoga ALK/Peresvet
Russia's Coastal Missile Shield - Bal-E & Bastion Mobile Coastal Cruise Missile Complexes
Iskander - Mobile Tactical Aero-Ballistic/Cruise Missile Complex
Russia's Strategic Missile Carrier/Bomber Roadmap 2018-2040 – PAK DA, Tu-160M2, Tu-95MSM & Tu-22M3M
Cold War Air Combats, USAF F-84E and Czechoslovak Air Force MiG-15 – West German Czechoslovak Border Region, 10 March 1952
XF-103: Mach 3 Mesospheric Interceptor Concept
Russian/Soviet Submarine Launched Ballistic Missiles, Nuclear Deterrence/Counter Force Strike
Ka-52/K Alligator/Katran, Scout (Reconnaissance)/Attack Helicopter
Sukhoi T-50/PAK FA - Russia's 5th Generation 'Stealth' Fighter
Sukhoi Su-35S 'Flanker' E - Russia's 4++ Generation Super-Manoeuvrability Fighter
Sukhoi Su-34 'Fullback'
Sukhoi Su-30MKK/MK2/M2 - Russo Kitashiy Striker from Amur
MiG-35/D 'Fulcrum' F – Towards the Fifth Generation
Air War over Syria, Tu-160, Tu-95MS & Tu-22M3 - Cruise Missile and Bombing Strikes on Syria, November 2015-February 2016
Sukhoi Su-27SM(3)/SKM
Russian/Soviet Aircraft Carrier & Carrier Aviation Design & Evolution Volume 1 - Seaplane Carriers, Project 71/72, Graf Zeppelin, Project 1123 ASW Cruiser & Project 1143-1143.4 Heavy Aircraft Carrying Cruiser
Raid on the Forth, The First German Air Raid on Great Britain in World War II
Light Battle Cruisers and the Second Battle of Heligoland Bight
Eurofighter Typhoon - Storm over Europe
North American F-108 Rapier - Mach 3 Interceptor
Convair YB-60 - Fort Worth Overcast
Boeing X-36 Tailless Agility Flight Research Aircraft
X-32 - The Boeing Joint Strike Fighter
X-35 - Progenitor to the F-35 Lightning II
X-45 Uninhabited Combat Air Vehicle
Hurricane IIB Combat Log - 151 Wing RAF, North Russia 1941
RAF Meteor Jet Fighters in World War II, an Operational Log

www.ingramcontent.com/pod-product-compliance
Lightning Source LLC
Chambersburg PA
CBHW081354040426
42450CB00016B/3443